TE DUE

THE ROCK CYCLE

by Rebecca Pettiford

Ideas for Parents and Teachers

Pogo Books let children practice reading informational text while introducing them to nonfiction features such as headings, labels, sidebars, maps, and diagrams, as well as a table of contents, glossary, and index.

Carefully leveled text with a strong photo match offers early fluent readers the support they need to succeed.

Before Reading

- "Walk" through the book and point out the various nonfiction features. Ask the student what purpose each feature serves.
- Look at the glossary together. Read and discuss the words.

Read the Book

- Have the child read the book independently.
- Invite him or her to list questions that arise from reading.

After Reading

- Discuss the child's questions. Talk about how he or she might find answers to those questions.
- Prompt the child to think more. Ask: What did you know about the rock cycle before you read this book? What more would you like to learn?

Pogo Books are published by Jump!
5357 Penn Avenue South
Minneapolis, MN 55419
www.jumplibrary.com

Library of Congress Cataloging-in-Publication Data

Names: Pettiford, Rebecca, author.
Title: The rock cycle / by Rebecca Pettiford.
Description: Minneapolis, MN: Jump!, Inc., [2018]
Series: Geology genius | Audience: Ages 7-10.
Includes bibliographical references and index.
Identifiers: LCCN 2017052359 (print)
LCCN 2017051351 (ebook)
ISBN 9781624968440 (ebook)
ISBN 9781624968426 (hardcover: alk. paper)
ISBN 9781624968433 (pbk.)
Subjects: LCSH: Petrology—Juvenile literature.
Geochemical cycles—Juvenile literature.
Classification: LCC QE432.2 (print)
LCC QE432.2 .P46 2018 (ebook) | DDC 552—dc23
LC record available at https://lccn.loc.gov/2017052359

Editor: Kristine Spanier
Book Designer: Michelle Sonnek
Content Consultant: Sandra Feher, M.S.G.E.

Photo Credits: All photos by Shutterstock except: Universal Images Group North America LLC/Alamy, 5 (Earth); ScottOrr/iStock, 19.

Printed in the United States of America at Corporate Graphics in North Mankato, Minnesota.

TABLE OF CONTENTS

CHAPTER 1

THE ROCK CYCLE BEGINS

Earth is always changing. Old rock breaks down. New rock forms. It is always being recycled.

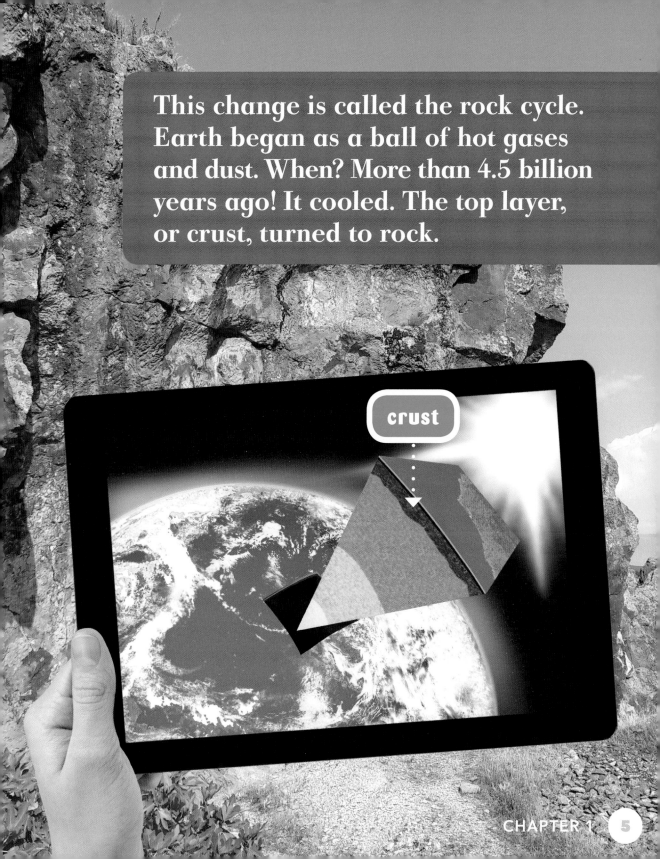

This change is called the rock cycle. Earth began as a ball of hot gases and dust. When? More than 4.5 billion years ago! It cooled. The top layer, or crust, turned to rock.

crust

Separate plates make up the crust. These plates are always moving. When they slide past each other, a **fault** is created. **Earthquakes** can occur here. When plates collide, **uplift** may occur. Mountains or **volcanoes** are made.

mountain

lava

The hot, liquid rock under Earth's crust is called magma. When plates are pushed apart, the magma can rise. It can cool beneath Earth and turn solid. Or it can reach the surface. How? Through **fissures** or volcanic eruptions. Then it is **lava**. It cools. New rock forms.

DID YOU KNOW?

The Ring of Fire is a chain of volcanoes. It is on the edge of the Pacific Ocean. It has more erupting volcanoes and earthquakes than any other place on Earth.

CHAPTER 2

TYPES OF ROCK

Three types of rock are in the rock cycle. Igneous. Sedimentary. Metamorphic. They are grouped by how they are formed. Each type of rock has **minerals** in it.

igneous rock

metamorphic rock

sedimentary rock

Minerals provide us with materials we use every day. Iron makes buildings strong. Copper is used in computers. Minerals make food healthier.

Igneous rock forms when magma cools and turns solid. This can happen above or below Earth. When magma cools quickly, it makes rock with small **crystals**. When it cools slowly, the crystals are larger.

DID YOU KNOW?

Granite is a kind of igneous rock. We use it to make monuments. An example is Mount Rushmore. It is in South Dakota.

igneous rock

sedimentary rock

Weathering and **erosion** break rock into small pieces called **sediment**. Wind and water move the sediment. The pieces gather in layers. Over time, they build up. Top layers **compact** the bottom layers. They **cement** together. Sedimentary rock forms.

DID YOU KNOW?

Sedimentary rock is easy to cut into blocks. It is frequently used in buildings.

Magma and uplift create intense heat and **pressure**. This can change all types of rock into metamorphic rock. Even metamorphic rock can transform again. The rock may fold. Minerals may change into different minerals.

metamorphic rock

TAKE A LOOK!

The rock cycle is not a perfect circle. All rock can turn into a different type of rock.

■ = melting
■ = cooling
■ = weathering and erosion
■ = heating and pressure
■ = compacting and cementing

SEDIMENT

SEDIMENTARY ROCK

IGNEOUS ROCK

METAMORPHIC ROCK

MAGMA

CHAPTER 3

ROCK TELLS A STORY

Rock covers Earth. It tells a story. When we study rock, we can learn about Earth's past. We can also understand its future.

How do we learn about life from the past? Plant and animal remains can get covered by sediment. They get cast in rock. These are called **fossils**. We study them. We learn about what once lived here.

fossil

Rock can tell us how Earth has reacted to **climate change**. This helps us understand how it affects us today. For example, seawater can **evaporate** in warm temperatures. It leaves behind a layer of salt. It appears in rock. Scientists study it. Will they learn something that can help us?

Go outside. Find a rock. Can you identify what kind of rock it is? What can it tell you about Earth?

ACTIVITIES & TOOLS

MAKE YOUR OWN ROCK CYCLE

Use crayons to see how the rock cycle works.

What You Need:
- 5 to 10 crayons
- cheese grater
- plate
- spoon
- paper cup
- microwave
- hot pad
- ice cube tray

❶ Remove the paper from the crayons. At this stage, the crayons are like igneous rocks. They are smooth and not mixed with anything else.

❷ Use the cheese grater to carefully grate the crayons onto a plate. Observe the crayon shavings. Mix the different colors together. These are like sediment.

❸ Press down on the shavings for one minute using a spoon. The shavings should stay together. This is like sedimentary rock.

❹ Press down on the shavings for a minute or two using the heat of your hand. Try folding the shavings together. This is like metamorphic rock.

❺ Put the shavings into a paper cup. With the help of an adult, microwave the shavings at medium heat for 30 seconds at a time until they fully melt.

❻ Remove the paper cup with a hot pad. Carefully pour the melted crayons into an empty ice cube tray. When the crayons cool, pop out the cubes. Observe them. They are now hard and smooth again. They have started over as igneous rock.

❼ Want to observe the rock cycle again? Repeat the steps using your new blocks of igneous rocks.

GLOSSARY

cement: To bind together and hold in place.

climate change: Global warming and other changes in the weather and weather patterns that are happening.

compact: To press or crush something together.

crystals: Repeating, three-dimensional arrangements of atoms or molecules.

earthquakes: Sudden, violent shakings of Earth.

erosion: To wear away from water, wind, heat, or ice.

evaporate: When a liquid changes into vapor or gas.

fault: A large break in Earth's surface that can cause an earthquake.

fissures: Narrow openings or cracks.

fossils: The remains, traces, or prints of plants or animals from the past that are preserved in rock.

lava: Hot, liquid rock that pours out of fissures or an erupting volcano.

minerals: Solid, natural substances with crystal structures, usually obtained from the ground.

pressure: The force produced by pressing on something.

sediment: Minerals, mud, gravel, or sand, or a combination of these, that have been carried to a place by water, wind, or glaciers.

uplift: To cause a portion of Earth's surface to rise above adjacent areas.

volcanoes: Mountains with openings through which molten lava, ash, and hot gases erupt.

weathering: The physical and chemical breakdown of materials at or near Earth's surface.

INDEX

TO LEARN MORE

Learning more is as easy as 1, 2, 3.

1) Go to www.factsurfer.com

2) Enter "rockcycle" into the search box.

3) Click the "Surf" button to see a list of websites.

With factsurfer, finding more information is just a click away.